Explorers & Exploration

The Travels of
Hernán Cortés

By Debbie Crisfield
Illustrated by Patrick O'Brien

Raintree Steck-Vaughn Publishers

A Harcourt Company

Austin · New York
www.steck-vaughn.com

Published by Raintree Steck-Vaughn Publishers, an imprint of Steck-Vaughn Company

Library of Congress Cataloging-in-Publication Data
Crisfield, Deborah
    Hernán Cortés/by Debbie Crisfield
        p. cm. — (Explorers and exploration)
    Includes index.
    Summary: A biography of the explorer whose brutal conquest of the Aztecs in Mexico was responsible for the first Spanish settlements in the New World.
    ISBN 0-7398-1488-5
    1. Cortés, Hernán, 1485–1547—Juvenile literature. 2. Mexico—History—Conquest—1519–1540—Juvenile literature. 3. Explorers—Mexico—Biography—Juvenile literature. 4. Explorers—Spain—Biography—Juvenile literature. 5. Conquerors—Mexico—Biography—Juvenile literature. [1. Cortés, Hernán, 1485–1547. 2. Explorers. 3. Mexico—History—Conquest, 1519–1540.] I. Title. II. Series.

F1230.C835 C75 2000
972'.02'092—dc21   99-054467

Printed in the United States of America
10 9 8 7 6 5 4 3 2 1 LB 03 02 01 00

Produced by By George Productions, Inc.

Illustration Acknowledgments:
p 5, Super Stock; pp 7, 24, 28, John Blazejewski; pp 11, 15, 26, 42, New York Public Library Picture Collection, p 20, Department of Library Services, American Museum of Natural History; pp 22–23, Stock Montage; p 32, John Carter Brown Library at Brown University. All other artwork is by Patrick O'Brien.

Contents

Getting to the Americas

The early 1500s was a time of change for the Age of Exploration. Before that time most explorers set off for special reasons. Some sailed to find new trade routes and draw maps. Some set out to bring Christianity to other lands. As the 1500s began, new kinds of explorers crossed the seas. They were "conquistadors," the Spanish word for conquerors. They wanted to take over other people's lands. Often they were cruel.

Hernán Cortés was a conqueror. With his soldiers, he destroyed the Aztec civilization, claiming Mexico for himself and Spain.

Although Cortés became a famous leader, he began life as a sickly child. He was born in Medellín, Spain, in 1485, to a family of good standing. By the time he was 14, he was healthy enough and smart enough for his family to send him to law school. But the teenaged Cortés was not a good student. It soon became clear to him that he did not like law. All he could think about were adventures in the land that would soon be known as the Americas. After two years of law school, Cortés quit to follow his dream.

His parents weren't pleased with his decision. But they helped him find a place on a ship heading across the Atlantic Ocean. Just before he was supposed to leave, he fell from a wall and was injured. Cortés was recovering when the ship sailed.

An old map showing the region Hernán Cortés would conquer

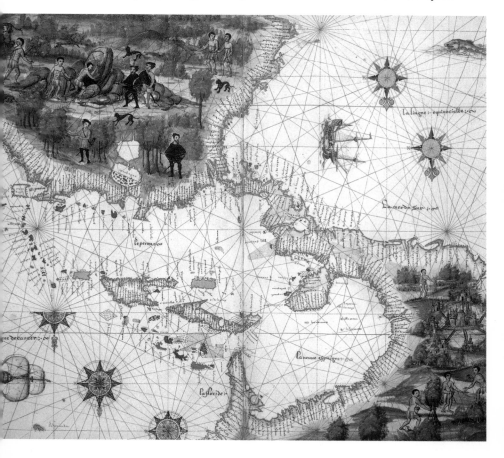

It took two more years for Cortés to make new plans. In 1504, Hernán Cortés at last crossed the Atlantic. He was 19 years old.

The trip across the ocean was not smooth. At one point Hernán thought that he would not make it, but he finally stepped ashore in the West. This was not the life he had planned for himself. When a man named Diego Velázquez was looking for people to join him on a trip to Cuba, Hernán wanted to go along.

The Spaniards attacked Cuba in 1511. Velázquez set himself up as governor of the island. Soon it became clear that not everyone was pleased with the way Velázquez was running things. Cortés and other men plotted against him. However, Velázquez had his spies. When Cortés tried to leave the island to make a report, Velázquez had him thrown in jail.

Cortés didn't stay in prison long. Experts are not sure how he got out. Some of them think he may have made friends with the jailer. Others think the jail may not have been very strong. Whatever the reason, Hernán got away. In a smart move, he went to a church. That was a place Velázquez would never dream of looking for him. But Velázquez could wait, and he did. As soon as Cortés tried to leave the church, he was arrested. Once again Cortés got away and returned to the church.

Hernán Cortés

This chase continued until a man named Juan Xuarez stepped in. Velázquez wanted to marry one of Xuarez's sisters, so Velázquez was willing to listen to this man. Cortés would listen to anyone who might help him out of this situation. Xuarez settled the quarrel. Experts are not sure how he did it. Cortés was set free, and soon he married Catalina, another of Juan's sisters. They settled down to a life on a farm, while Cortés kept looking for more adventures.

Some of the treasures that were to be found in a place called Mexico

Off to Mexico

By 1518 word had spread about a land to the west of Cuba. People said there were mountains of gold in this place they called Mexico. A small group had visited and brought back gold that they'd gotten from trading with the native peoples. Velázquez was eager to claim this rich land for Spain. He decided to send a larger expedition. The 34-year-old Cortés wanted to be its leader. Cortés had quite a few friends on the island, and his relations with Velázquez had improved. He got the job.

Cortés wasted no time. Using much of his own money, he began to gather ships and men. His excitement spread to almost everyone on the island, except Velázquez. Velázquez started to worry that Cortés wanted to make himself a ruler. He decided that Cortés should not be the leader of the expedition.

However, Velázquez never had a chance to replace Cortés. This time Cortés had spies of his own. As soon as word of Velázquez's plans became known, Cortés knew he had to act quickly. Even though he wasn't finished preparing, he told his men that they were leaving in the morning. True to his word, Cortés sailed from the port at dawn.

Because they had left so quickly, the ships weren't fully supplied. Over the next year Cortés stopped at islands along the way to reload the ships. Some of his men had already been to Mexico. One of them was named Pedro de Alvarado. He became Cortés's second in command. Finally, in 1519, with 11 ships and about 600 men, Hernán Cortés reached Mexico.

Cortés marches into Mexico.

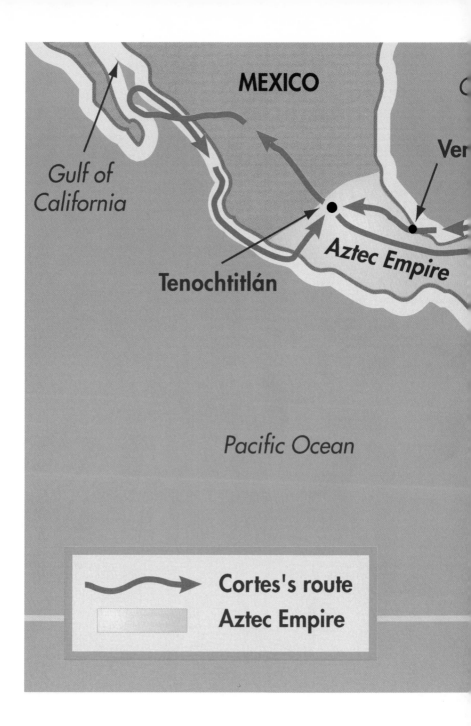

MEXICO

Ver

Gulf of
California

Aztec Empire

Tenochtitlán

Pacific Ocean

Cortes's route
Aztec Empire

12 ◡◡◡

Mexico

Caribbean Sea

CUBA

Santiago
de Cuba

Cozumel

Trujillo

Caribbean Sea

SOUTH
AMERICA

Equator

13

Princess Marina

Most of the native peoples in Mexico did not welcome these newest visitors. Earlier meetings with other Spaniards had taught them that their way of life was not safe around these men. Although Cortés had not expected to go into battle so soon, he was prepared to fight. Using guns and cannons, Cortés's army overcame the native peoples. The Spaniards moved quickly ahead.

In Cozumel, Cortés found a translator, a person who can change words from one language into another. His name was Aguilar. He was a Spaniard who had been put in prison years earlier. There he had learned the Mayan language. Mayan land covered much of the southern part of Mexico. Through Aguilar, Cortés was able to talk to the Mayans he met and make peace with them.

Malinche, once an Aztec princess, was named Marina by the Spaniards.

One of these meetings was very useful. As a peace offering, a native chief gave Cortés and his men 20 slave women. One of these women was named Malinche.

Malinche had many names. Born Malinali, she was named Malinche by the Maya. Malinche had been an Aztec princess. She had led an easy life in the lands to the north, training to be a leader.

The princess had been a child when her father, the king, died years earlier. Malinali had expected that she would rule the Aztecs herself when she was old enough. Her mother had other plans. She had married again and had a son by her second husband. Malinali's mother wanted this son to be king. When Malinali was 12, her mother had her sold to a Mayan group far to the south. It was this group that called her Malinche and then gave her to Cortés.

By this time, the former princess was a young woman. The Spaniards renamed her Marina. She was to become very helpful to Cortés. She spoke both the Aztec and Mayan languages. Between Aguilar and Marina, Cortés could talk with almost every native group in Mexico.

Cortés would talk to Aguilar in Spanish. Aguilar would change the Spanish to Mayan. Then Marina would change the Mayan to the

Aztec language. It was difficult, but it worked. Because Marina learned so quickly, she began to speak Spanish as well. Soon Aguilar was out of a job.

But Marina became much more than Cortés's translator. She also let Cortés know what the Aztecs were thinking. With this information, Cortés was able to conquer the Aztecs more easily.

The Aztecs were a people who knew science, art, building, and farming. Many of the Aztecs were good jewelers and weavers, and they had invented their own picture writing. Some people blamed Marina for letting her people down. But it is easy to understand why she did not like the Aztecs.

Meeting with the Aztecs

By now word of Cortés and his army had reached the Aztec emperor, Montezuma. An emperor is the ruler of a large territory. The reports told of houses on the water (ships) and thunder weapons (guns and cannons). They told of deer that carried men (horses) and people with white skin and yellow hair.

Montezuma didn't know what to think. On the one hand, he worried that these people were a danger that should be fought off. On the other hand, astrologers, or people who study stars, had said there would be an attack that would lead to the fall of the Aztec Empire. Montezuma knew of Cortés's battles with native groups to the south. Was Cortés a man to be feared?

The Aztec emperor, Montezuma, did not know what to expect when Cortés arrived.

But Montezuma also wondered if Cortés was actually the Aztec god Quetzalcoatl. In Aztec legend, this light-skinned god had sailed from Mexico across the sea but would return one day. Montezuma certainly didn't want to attack and anger a god.

So Montezuma came up with a plan. He sent Cortés gifts of gold and a message asking that Cortés's army go home. Montezuma's plan did not work. As soon as Cortés saw the gold, he wanted more. And he wanted to see the city where all these beautiful gold pieces had been made. Also, Marina was able to tell Cortés all about Montezuma's beliefs. Cortés knew that if the Aztec leader believed he was a god, then Cortés had little to fear.

Cortés meets Montezuma for the first time.

So the Spaniards moved on toward the Aztecs and Montezuma. Along the way Cortés met many native groups. He found that most of the nearby groups hated the Aztecs. The Aztec religion called for humans to be sacrificed to the gods every day. They believed this kept the gods strong. Rather than kill their own people, the Aztecs went to nearby groups to get people to sacrifice. These peoples were happy to join with Cortés in a war against the Aztecs.

Montezuma sent gifts of gold to Cortés.

Velázquez's ships arrive at Veracruz.

Burning the Ships

Cortés's men were starting to complain. Some of them had died of malaria, a disease spread by mosquitoes. Many others were sick. Why not head home? They had already taken bundles of gold and treasures from the Aztecs and other local groups. They would be rich men when they returned to Cuba.

Cortés warned the men that Velázquez would take a large part of the treasure, which rulers often did. The men wouldn't be left with much. Cortés insisted that they needed more treasure.

Most of the men were convinced. The ones who were not were taken prisoner. Though there was grumbling among his men, Cortés knew that he had to conquer the Aztecs. He couldn't go back.

Cortés continued to sail up the coast. He landed near the city that is now called Veracruz. Cortés decided to set up a colony of his own there. This was something else that Velázquez wouldn't like. Setting up a colony was not part of the mission.

Cortés knew that at some point he would need a friend who was powerful. So he sent many of his Aztec treasures directly to the king of Spain rather than sending them to Velázquez, who would then send them to the king.

Some of the soldiers were not pleased with the way Cortés was running things. A group of men grabbed one of the ships and sailed back to Cuba. Cortés was angry. He couldn't let this happen again. To prevent it, he burned all but one of the ships. The Spaniards were left in Mexico, with no choice but to support Cortés.

Cortés himself ordered his ships to be burned.

Cortés arrives in Tenochtitlán in 1519.

In the Aztec Capital

Cortés and his men finally made it to the Aztec capital of Tenochtitlán late in 1519. This great city was built in the middle of a lake. There were causeways, or bridges, leading out to it. Many of the streets were canals. Canals are waterways that are dug across land. Never in their lives had the Spaniards seen anything so unusual and grand.

Though Cortés had 500 Spaniards and thousands of native people on his side, the Aztecs had even more soldiers. Montezuma thought that Cortés might be the god Quetzalcoatl. Because of this, Cortés was allowed to march right into the city. He was allowed to speak with the great emperor Montezuma at once.

At first the meetings between the two leaders went well. Cortés announced that he came in peace. He let the Aztecs believe that he was the Aztec god. Montezuma let Cortés do anything he wanted. He gave Cortés and his men all the food and treasures they desired.

Peace lasted for a few days. But the more the Spaniards saw of the Aztec way of life, the less they liked it. The Spaniards were Christians. The religion of the Aztecs seemed completely wrong to them.

In addition, the Spaniards were getting more greedy for gold and treasures. They wanted everything. So not long after his peaceful arrival, Cortés had his men capture Montezuma and hold him prisoner. The Aztecs did not attack. Experts think this may be because they believed that Cortés was the god Quetzalcoatl.

In spite of being a prisoner, Montezuma continued to rule through the Spaniards for months. Things were somewhat peaceful during that time. When Cortés learned of trouble back in Veracruz, he left the now-quiet Aztec city. Just before he returned to Veracruz, Cortés left his second in command, Pedro de Alvarado, in charge.

Alvarado did not keep peace while Cortés was away. During an Aztec religious feast, all the Aztecs were dancing and not armed. Alvarado ordered his men to move in and kill them. The soldiers did so.

Aztecs wore armor like this.

The Aztecs fought back and trapped the Spaniards in the palace. When Cortés returned, he was locked in there as well. Montezuma was killed in the battle. Some say his own people killed him.

The Spaniards knew they didn't have enough soldiers. They would not be able to fight their way out of the city. They decided to slip out at night, in the dark. But luck was not with them. The Aztecs were waiting for them and attacked.

Many of the Spaniards tried to jump into the lake and swim for shore. But their greed had gotten the best of them. When they sneaked out, they tried to take the Aztec treasures with them. In the water, the heavy gold that they had hidden on their bodies quickly dragged them to the bottom of the lake. Many men drowned. Only a quarter of Cortés's men made it out of the city alive. Cortés was one of them.

The Spaniards tried to leave the Aztec city at night.

The Return

Cortés would not accept defeat. It took him almost a year, but he gathered the groups of native peoples who had sided with him before and returned to Tenochtitlán in May 1521. This time he stopped just outside the city. His plan of attack was simple. Because he still didn't have enough men, Cortés couldn't fight the Aztecs the way an army usually did. He had to cut off the city in the lake from all of its supplies.

His first move was to destroy the aqueducts, which brought fresh water into the city. Then he circled the city and cut off the causeways. After that the Aztecs couldn't leave or bring in food.

Cortés's soldiers wore armor like this during their battles with native peoples.

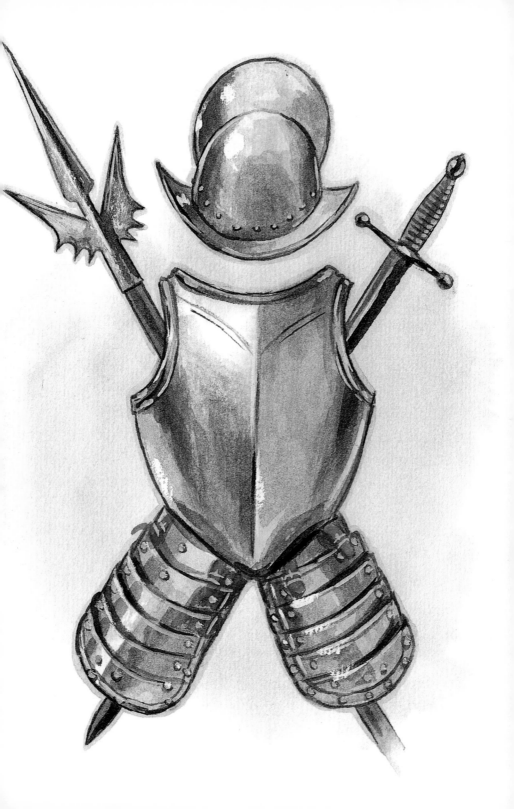

Cortés's plan worked. Many Aztecs died from lack of food and water. However, many Aztecs also died of the terrible disease of smallpox while Cortés was keeping them trapped in the city. The Spaniards had brought this disease and others with them a year earlier without even knowing it. The Spanish were able to fight the diseases because their bodies were used to them. The Aztecs died from the diseases.

After about three months, the Spaniards figured out how weak the Aztecs had become. Cortés and his men moved in on the city. They moved slowly, destroying everything in their way. They knocked down buildings and temples to fill in the canals, so the army could march. They destroyed statues of the Aztec gods because they went against the Spaniards' Christian beliefs. And they killed any Aztecs who tried to fight them. In August the Aztec leader surrendered.

In the end very few Aztec people were left. Cortés had brought about the death of more than 300,000 Aztecs. With this came the end of their entire civilization and way of life.

The Spaniards destroyed several Aztec temples.

The Final Years

Cortés and his men took all the Aztec treasures they could find. But their riches fell far short of what they expected. There were stories, but never any proof, about the Aztec treasures. Some said that the Aztecs sank as many treasures as they could while they were being starved in their city. Little was left of Tenochtitlán, the ruins of which now lie beneath Mexico City.

It was a terrible end to a powerful civilization. And all this ruin came at the hands of a small army led by Hernán Cortés.

Cortés was a bold conqueror who became the Spanish ruler of Mexico.

After the Aztecs were defeated, Cortés was, without question, the ruler of Mexico. His army moved through the land, destroying temples and statues. The Spaniards spread the Christian religion by force. They felt they were doing the right thing.

The Spaniards also made slaves of the native peoples and then claimed their land. The native peoples who lived on the land were thought of as slaves of the new "owners" of the land. Cortés himself claimed land that covered more than 25,000 square miles (64,700 sq km). This is larger than the entire state of West Virginia.

In 1528 Cortés returned to Spain for the first time since he had left at the age of 19. He received a hero's welcome and was given land and titles. But he didn't get what he really wanted: the title of Governor of Mexico. Disappointed, Cortés returned to the Americas, which was now under the rule of someone appointed by the king. And slowly the king made up his mind that Cortés was not a hero after all.

Though Cortés had won large new lands for Spain and had sent back a fortune in gold, he fell out of favor with the king. In 1540 Cortés left Mexico. He sailed back to Spain to fight for his rights and his good name. But now the king wouldn't even listen to him.

Cortés fought in the Spanish courts for years. But he knew that he was getting older. He decided he wanted to die in the land that he had fought for and won. He was on his way to Seville to go back to Mexico when he died on December 2, 1547. He was 62 years old.

Cortés burned Velazquez's ships at Veracruz.

Other Events of the 16th Century
(1501 – 1600)

During the century that Cortés was exploring Mexico, events were happening in other parts of the world. Some of these were:

1502   Portuguese navigator Vasco da Gama makes his second voyage to India in order to expand trade.

1520   Ferdinand Magellan, the Portuguese navigator, sails around the southern tip of South America.

1524   Giovanni da Verrazano, an Italian sailor, explores the coast of North America from North Carolina to Maine.

1534   Francisco Pizarro of Spain conquers the Inca Empire in Peru.

1541   John Calvin spreads Protestantism in France.

Time Line

1485	Hernán Cortés is born.
1499	Cortés is sent to law school.
1501	Cortés quits law school and finds a place on a ship bound for the New World. An injury keeps him from going.
1503	Cortés boards a ship bound for the West Indies.
1511	Velázquez conquers Cuba with Cortés at his side.
1513–1514	After a continuing quarrel with Velázquez, Cortés marries Catalina Xuarez and settles down to a life on the farm.
1518	Velázquez decides an expedition should be sent to Mexico with Cortés in command.
March 1519	Cortés reaches Mexico.

June 1519	Cortés burns his ships.
November 1519	Montezuma and Cortés meet for the first time.
May 1520	Alvarado orders the killing of Aztecs while Cortés is away.
June 1520	The Spaniards try to escape from Tenochtitlán, and many of them die.
1521	After three months of Tenochtitlán being surrounded, the Aztec Empire falls to Cortés.
1528	Cortés returns to Spain for the first time since he left at age 19 and is hailed a hero.
1530	Cortés returns to Mexico.
1540	Cortés returns to Spain to fight to be recognized as governor of Mexico.
1547	Cortés dies while planning his return to the Americas.

Glossary

Aguilar (ah-GWEEL-ar) A Spaniard who had learned the Mayan language and became a translator for Cortés

aqueduct (AK-weh-duct) A structure for carrying large amounts of water

astrologer (az-TROL-oh-jer) One who studies the supposed effects of the stars on both humans and life on Earth

canals Waterways dug across land

causeway (KAWZ-way) Raised path across wet ground or water

colony (KOL-uh-nee) An area that has been settled by people from one country and is governed by that country

conquistador (kun-KEES-tuh-dor) The Spanish word for "conqueror"

de Alvarado, Pedro (day al-vahr-AHD-oh, PAID-row) Cortés's second in command during his expedition to Mexico

emperor The ruler of a large territory

empire A large territory that is under the rule of one leader

expedition (ek-spuh-DISH-un) A journey for a special purpose, such as to explore or take over lands

fleet A group of ships under one command

malaria (muh-LAYR-ee-uh) A disease spread by mosquitoes and characterized by high fever

Malinche (mahl-EEN-chay) A woman owned by Cortés who was once an Aztec princess

Mayans (MY-uhns) An Indian civilization in the southern part of Mexico

Montezuma (mont-ay-ZOOM-ah) The last emperor of the Aztecs

Quetzalcoatl (ket-zuhl-KOE-at-uhl) An Aztec god

smallpox A deadly, catching disease that affects the skin

Tenochtitlán (ten-oash-teet-LUHN) The Aztec capital, now Mexico City

Velázquez, Diego (vel-AHZ-kays, dee-EG-oh) Governor of Cuba and the leader of the expedition to that island.

Xuarez, Juan (WORE-ez, wahn) A man who settled a feud between Hernán Cortés and Diego Velázquez

Index